SOMETHING TO CHEW ON

❸❶Days of Faith Confessions

SOMETHING TO CHEW ON

31 Days of Faith Confessions

PASTOR CARL SHEGOG

COOKE HOUSE
PUBLISHING
WINSTON SALEM

SOMETHING TO CHEW ON:
31 DAYS OF FAITH CONFESSIONS
Copyright © 2017 – Carl Shegog

Soft cover ISBN: 978-0-9979923-8-0

Cooke House Publishing
(a division of Cooke Consulting & Creations, LLC)
Winston-Salem, NC
publishing@cookecc.org

This book and all Cooke House Publishing books are available at Christian bookstores and distributors worldwide.

Printed in the United States of America.- First Edition

CONTENTS

DEDICATION

This book is dedicated first to my Lord and Savior Jesus Christ, without whom none of this would be possible.

I give a special thanks to my wonderful, awesome, beautiful wife, Pastor Valarie. Thank you for being there for me. You have encouraged and inspired me to push forward. You are the best thing that God has ever given me and I honor you with this book. For 36 years you have been my helper. Thank you so much.

To my dad and mom, Mr. George Shegog Jr. and Mrs. Annie Margaret Shegog, you have taught me so much in life that will forever be with me. Even with your move to heaven I miss you dearly.

Ms. Doris Hoskins, I love you for allowing me to marry your daughter. I will always remember your gift of wisdom.

To my brothers and sisters. It's true, blood is thicker than water.

To Apostles Tony and Cynthia Brazelton. Your guidance in my life means the world to me. You have taken the role of being my dad and mom and I'm forever grateful.

Elders Morris and Yolanda Goins, thanks for being on my strongest flank. Your love and support is dear to my heart.

To the best church family in the world, Word Alive Family Worship Center, you are the best. What an honor it is to be your Pastor.

Day 1

Declare by Faith, I Will Do It Again

Philippians 4:4 (ERV)

Always be filled with joy in the Lord. I will say it again. Be filled with joy.

Being filled with joy when you are going through a difficult time is not always easy to do, especially when you receive a bad report from the doctor or there is trouble in your marriage. Rejoicing is the last thing you want to do. But to God it is our first step of action. When the enemy tries to send you thoughts of giving up, just remind yourself that you're filled with the joy of the Lord. Keep repeating until the peace of God floods your spirit. Your strength comes from Who you know not what you know.

Declaration:

I declare that my joy tank will stay full of God's joy. In the name of Jesus, devil you can't have my peace. This is the day that my Lord has made and I will rejoice and be glad in it. God's mercy and grace are new every morning in my life and my family. In Jesus' name, so be it.

Day 2

Strength to Keep Moving

1 John 4:4 (ERV)

My children, you belong to God, so you have already defeated these false prophets. That's because the one who is in you is greater than the one who is in the world.

When things seem to get hard remember that there is a greater force inside of you that will push you toward your purpose. Greater is He that is in you than he that is in the world. As long as you keep moving forward, your faith will go as well. No matter what it looks like, declare by faith, "I'm going to make it." Declare by faith that it's already done.

Declaration:

In the name of Jesus, I declare that victory belongs to me. Father, because Your spirit lives in me, I am strong and powerful. The same spirit that raised Jesus from the dead lives in me. Therefore, I have overcoming faith. I declare nothing is too hard for You. Because You defeated death I am victorious over it as well. I declare that I will live and not die because you have given me long life. I will not fear because man can't touch me. I belong to You; therefore, I am a winner. Thank you, Jesus. I receive this by faith. In Jesus' name, Amen.

Day 3

Restoration of Everything

Deuteronomy 30:3-13 (MSG)

God, your God, will restore everything you lost; he'll have compassion on you; he'll come back and pick up the pieces from all the places where you were scattered. No matter how far away you end up, God, your God, will get you out of there and bring you back to the land your ancestors once possessed. It will be yours again. He will give you a good life and make you more numerous than your ancestors. God, your God, will cut away the thick calluses on your heart and your children's hearts, freeing you to love God, your God, with your whole heart and soul and live, really live. God, your God, will put all these curses on your enemies who hated you and were out to get you. And you will make a new start, listening obediently to God, keeping all his commandments that I'm commanding you today. God, your God, will outdo himself in making things go well for you: you'll have babies, get calves, grow crops, and enjoy an all-around good life. Yes, God will start enjoying you again, making things go well for you just as he enjoyed doing it for your ancestors.

But only if you listen obediently to God, your God, and keep the commandments and regulations written in this Book of Revelation. Nothing halfhearted here; you must return to God, your God, totally, heart and soul, holding nothing back.

This commandment that I'm commanding you today isn't too much for you, it's not out of your reach. It's not on a high mountain—you don't have to get mountaineers to climb the peak and bring it down to your level and explain it before you can live it. And it's not across the ocean—you don't have to send sailors out to get it, bring it back, and then explain it before you can live it. No. The word is right here and now—as near as the tongue in your mouth, as near as the heart in your chest. Just do it!

Whenever God makes a promise you can be sure that it will come to pass. Think about what has happened in your life that you need God to restore. Because God is a God of compassion He is going to restore everything that has been stolen. No matter how far you have fallen, He is able to pick you up. Whatever the enemy has thrown at you to cause your heart to be hardened towards God, God Himself will cut it away from you. Make out your list and place it before the feet of Jesus. If you ask the Father anything, He said He'll do it. A brand new start awaits you on the other side of your obedience. You have the word of God to create your world. So start today and confess that whatever the devil has stolen will be returned to me one-hundred fold. The last part of this verse is so powerful. It says. "Just do it." Declare that today you will JUST DO IT.

Declaration:

I declare by faith that whatever is missing in my life God is about to restore it. My life is going to get better. My marriage, family, and children will be better. My health will be restored. My finances and job will get better. My home will be better. My love walk will be better. My giving and receiving will be better. My business will get better. Everything around me is going to be better. I declare by faith that because God loves me, He will outdo Himself on my behalf. In the name of Jesus, I declare that restoration has come to my house. In Jesus' name, Amen.

Day 4

Your Daddy is Listening

1 John 5:14 (MSG)

My purpose in writing is simply this: that you who believe in God's Son will know beyond the shadow of a doubt that you have eternal life, the reality and not the illusion. And how bold and free we then become in his presence, freely asking according to his will, sure that he's listening. And if we're confident that he's listening, we know that what we've asked for is as good as ours.

I can remember asking my mother for something while she was cooking. Growing up in the south you never disturbed mama while she was cooking. I repeated my question again because I thought she did not hear me the first time. To my surprise she said, "Boy, I heard you!"

Remember this: no matter how long it takes for your promise to come just know your Daddy is listening and that He heard you. Get ready, it's on the way.

Declaration:

I declare that every word I have prayed by faith it will come to pass. I release my faith that my Daddy is listening to my every word. And what He has promise will come to pass. In Jesus name, Amen.

Day 5

All is Well with Me

3 John 2 (ERV)

My dear friend, I know that you are doing well spiritually. So I pray that everything else is going well with you and that you are enjoying good health.

When we are challenged with health issues, family issues, or money problems, we can forget that God is there with us. But He promised that no matter what He is there. When you look through the eyes of faith you will see yourself the way God sees you. He sees you healed and blessed. God is still writing your story. And the truth of the matter is that your story has a happy ending. So, wake up every morning and say good things about yourself. Say what God's word has to say about your problem. If it's a money problem, say God will provide all of my need. If it's healing, say by His stripes I'm healed. Whatever your issue may be, the word of God has a solution for it. No matter what your problem may be, confess by faith that everything will be well. And when you release your faith, stand and don't change your position. Remember, this too shall pass.

Declaration:

I declare by faith that all is well with me. I release my faith and say I am blessed. I am healed. Everything will be well with me. I declare that as Jesus is, so am I in this world. In Jesus name, Amen.

Day 6

Yes Lord, I Believe

1 John 5:4 (MSG)

Every God-begotten person conquers the world's ways. The conquering power that brings the world to its knees is our faith. The persons who wins over the world's ways is simple the one who believes Jesus is the Son of God.

What a wonderful promise from God that He has given us. Your faith is so powerful that it can defeat whatever is trying to come against you. Our faith is designed to bring the things of this world to its knees. You have the God-given ability to bring sickness to its knees. You have the God-given ability to bring whatever is in the world system to its knees.

Declaration:

I declare by faith that I believe I have God-given ability at this moment. And God's ability is the power of His spoken Word. In the name of Jesus, I declare I have the same ability to speak the word of faith out of my mouth and to bring the world system to its knees. Because of that power, I am victorious in every area of my life. I am more than a conqueror. By faith, I am a world overcomer. I overcome by the blood of the Lamb and the word of my testimony. In the name of Jesus, it's my faith in God and faith in His word that allows me to have victory over this world. Shout, "Lord, I believe!"

Day 7

Go All Out for Each Other

Ephesians 5:25 25-28 (MSG)

Husbands, go all out in your love for your wives, exactly as Christ did for the church—a love marked by giving, not getting. Christ's love makes the church whole. His words evoke her beauty. Everything he does and says is designed to bring the best out of her, dressing her in dazzling white silk, radiant with holiness. And that is how husbands ought to love their wives. They're really doing themselves a favor—since they're already "one" in marriage.

Marriage can be hard if we do not place Christ in the center of it. One night, I was praying to God and thanking Him for everything He has done and doing in our lives. The Lord spoke these words to me: "You can't change what you did not create." Many times, we want to change our spouse and that is not our job. Our part is to submit and walk in love. It's easy to get frustrated when one expectation is not met. Whatever it may be in your marriage that is causing you to become frustrated, take it to JESUS.

Declaration:

I declare by faith that my love for my spouse is stronger than ever. We are one and the same. I cover my spouse with the washing of the Word of God. The blood of Jesus is our protection against the evil one and no plots will work against us. We speak the word of faith over our marriage and declare that we walk in divine favor and blessing. We are blessed in our union. We allow the Word of God and our walk with the lord to be our guide that will draw others to Christ. In the name of Jesus, we have a strong marriage and from this day forward we will go all out in our love for each other. In Jesus' name, Amen.

Day 8

Can't Do It Without You

Genesis 2:18 (ERV)

Then the Lord God said, "I see that it is not good for the man to be alone. I will make the companion he needs, one just right for him."

God has graced our marriage union 36 years. My wife, Pastor Valarie, has always been in my corner to encourage me and to push me toward my dreams. She has been there every step of my walk of faith. All of my success is because of her support. She told me from the first day, "Honey I am your biggest fan." My heart skips a beat every time I see her. There is nothing like having a strong woman by your side. God made her for me. She is just right for me.

Husband, your wife is a gift to you from God. Determine in your mind today that your wife's assignment is to help you. You have to receive what God has given you. When she brings something to you, open up your heart and receive what God has given her. You wife is anointed. She is just right for you.

Declaration:

I declare by faith that my wife is a gift from God to me. Her assignment is to help me with whatever it is that You have given me to do. Father, in the Name of Jesus, I thank you for sending me help. I declare that my wife is well capable, intelligent, patient, and virtuous. My wife is far more precious than jewels and her value to me and our family is far above rubies and pearls. Thank you, Lord, that my wife is filled with wisdom, skills, kindness, and love. My children rise up and declare we are blessed and happy. I declare by faith that my wife has the power to carry out Proverbs 31:10-31. I declare that I can't do without her. In Jesus' name, Amen.

Day 9

Embrace the Word

Mark 11:22-25 (MSG)

Jesus was matter-of-fact: "Embrace this God-life. Really embrace it, and nothing will be too much for you. This mountain, for instance: Just say, 'Go jump in the lake'—no shuffling or shilly-shallying—and it's as good as done. That's why I urge you to pray for absolutely everything, ranging from small to large. Include everything as you embrace this God-life, and you'll get God's everything. And when you assume the posture of prayer, remember that it's not all asking. If you have anything against someone, forgive—only then will your heavenly Father be inclined to also wipe your slate clean of sins

In this walk of faith, we will all encounter some not so good days. But what do you do at that moment? We have two choices: we can say what our problem is or we can declare what the Word of God says. Your first words are important. When we feel sick the first thing we may say is that I am coming down with something. It may be a fact but it's not the truth. Truth will always override facts. Instead, you say I am healed by the stripes of Jesus. Sickness has no power over me, therefore, because of Jesus' broken body and the stripes that wounded Him, I am healed.

Declaration:

I declare by faith that I will embrace the Word of God and speak the word only over my life and the life of my loved ones. When I say what God said and believe that word, I now can have whatsoever I say because my words have creative power. I will say what my Father says and when I do that what I ask for will be granted to me. In Jesus' name, Amen.

Day 10

Payday is Coming

Joel 2:25 (ERV)

I, the Lord, sent my army against you. The swarming locusts and the hopping locusts and the destroying locusts and the cutting locusts ate everything you had. But I will pay you back for those years of trouble.

It's payday time for the body of Christ. God has the best payday system in the world. Begin to declare that payday is coming to my house.

Declaration:

I declare by faith that the God of the breakthrough is coming to my house. I declare my payday is now. I declare that every trouble in my life will be replaced with peace. I declare that my God will bring back into existence, reestablish, put things back in order, and bring me into my wealthy place. I position myself as God brings restitution of anything taken away or lost. This is my payday season!

Day 11

Victory Belongs to You

1 Peter 5:7 (ERV)

Give all your worries to him, because he cares for you.

Fear comes to force out in our heart what God has spoken over us. If we are not watching what goes in our ear gate, our eye gate, and out of our mouth, the enemy will begin to plant a seed of fear through what is taking place in our lives that will drain and rob us of the peace that God has given us. Make a quality decision today that I will not take fear of any kind. For example, when bills arrive and you are unsure how you will pay them, say, "Lord, you have mail." Give them over to Him and watch Him work the victory.

Declaration:

I declare that I am free from the spirit of fear. Fear is from the enemy. Therefore, I refuse to give place to fear. My God has given me His power so I have no reason to fear. Because God is on my side, I walk in complete victory in every area of my life. Therefore, I cast all my concerns upon Him. I declare as of today I have no concerns. In Jesus' name, Amen.

Day 12

What are You Eating?

Proverb 18:20-21 (ERV)

Your words can be as satisfying as fruit, as pleasing as the food that fills your stomach. The tongue can speak words that bring life or death. Those who love to talk must be ready to accept what it brings.

This is such a powerful verse. The last sentence is powerful. "Those who love to talk must be ready to accept what it brings." Have you ever noticed someone who loves to talk? You can tell a lot about a person by listening to what they are saying. If you want to bring good things in your life then the words that you decide to eat today will for sure determine the harvest that will come in your life. You are a product of what you eat. Chew on His word; it is filled with what you need.

Declaration:

I declare by faith that only good words come out of my mouth. God has given me the power to create my world. Therefore, I will speak the Word of God only. My words shape my life and my future. In the name of Jesus, I feast on God's word to bring to pass what I need. I declare that all of my needs are meet and I lack nothing. In Jesus' name, Amen.

Day 13

Time of Rest

Matthew 11:28 (ERV)

*Come to me all of you who are tired from the heavy burden you
have been forced to carry. I will give you rest.*

Here is a request that we can't turn down. Jesus wants us to
come to Him when things are not going well. Another
translation says, "Come to me all who are heavy laden." The
image that comes to mind when using the term 'heavy laden' is
of someone who is carrying such a heavy load on his or her back
that it is causing them pain. What are you carrying that is causing
you pain?

Declaration:

I declare today that I will rest in the presence of God. Father, I
come to you in the name of Jesus. I have carried this pain for the
last day. I bring to you everything that is causing me pain. Today,
I take my position at Your feet to rest. I know that You will never
leave or forsake me. Therefore, it is by faith that I rest in You. In
Jesus' name, Amen.

Day 14

He Will

Psalm 91:1-13 (ERV)

You can go to God Most High to hide.
You can go to God All-Powerful for protection.
I say to the LORD, "YOU ARE MY PLACE OF SAFETY, MY FORTRESS.
My God, I trust in you."
God will save you from hidden dangers
and from deadly diseases.
You can go to him for protection.
He will cover you like a bird spreading its wings over its
babies.
You can trust him to surround and protect you like a shield.
You will have nothing to fear at night
and no need to be afraid of enemy arrows during the day.
You will have no fear of diseases that come in the dark
or terrible suffering that comes at noon.
A thousand people may fall dead at your side
or ten thousand right beside you,
but nothing bad will happen to you!
All you will have to do is watch,
and you will see that the wicked are punished.
You trust in the LORD FOR PROTECTION.
You have made God Most High your place of safety.
So nothing bad will happen to you.
No diseases will come near your home.
He will command his angels to protect you wherever you go.
Their hands will catch you
so that you will not hit your foot on a rock.
You will have power to trample on lions
and poisonous snakes.

It's so awesome to know that you can trust someone. You can always call on Jesus. He will always be there for you. As you go throughout your day, take some time to talk with God. His ears are open to you. Lean not to your own way of doing things but in all of your ways acknowledge Him and He will surely guide you.

Decide today that you will trust Jesus. Whenever we call upon God He is always there to help us. When you think about how big your God is there is nothing to be afraid of. God's name carries so much weight. Whatever you need Him to be in your life, He can become it. If you need protection, He can be that. If you need a place from your enemies, He is your refuge. God will be your personal bodyguard. Because of His love for you He will never fail you. Take the time today to mediate on this powerful promise from God the Father in Psalm 91.

Declaration:

I declare by faith that my God is watching over me every day. He is my refuge in time of trouble. Lord, my faith and trust is in you. In Jesus' name, Amen.

Day 15

Go Ahead and Say So

Psalm 107:1-2 (ERV)

Praise the Lord, because he is good! His faithful love will last forever!

Everyone the Lord has saved should repeat that word of thanks. Praise him, all who have been rescued from the enemy.

Nothing will take place in your lives without the spoken Word of God. Most people are where they are now because of wrong words they have spoken. If you don't like where you are, change what you say. Remember, YOU have what YOU say. Speak the word only. When problems arise, speak the word only. When you receive a bad report from the doctor, speak the word only. The angels harken to the voice of the word that you speak. Your angels are on assignment to carry out what you say. So, make sure you are saying the right words. Make sure that you put your angels to work today.

Declaration:

I declare by faith that God is faithful to me and His mercy never ends. I will say I am blessed. I say I am healed. I say I have been rescued from those who mean me harm. Father, in the name of Jesus, I will give you praise now and forever because You have been so good to me. I say so today, that I am saved from every attack of the enemy. In Jesus' name, Amen.

Day 16

The Great Exchange

Matthew 23:23 (ERV)

It will be bad for you teachers of the law and you Pharisees!
You are hypocrites! You give God a tenth of the food you get,
even your mint, dill, and cumin. But you don't obey the really
important teachings of the law—being fair, showing mercy,
and being faithful. These are the things you should do. And you
should also continue to do those other things.

It's a true saying that where your heart is so will your treasures
lie. Where is your heart when it comes to giving? You can tell
where a person's heart is when you take a look at their checkbook.
Today is the day of new beginning. God's Word is true and it has
passed the test. God will never force you to give. Giving has to
do with the attitude of the heart. Giving is a sincere proof of your
love for God. Settle in your heart today that you will give to God
that which is His.

Declaration:

I declare that I am a sower, and because I am a sower I will always
have seed to sow. Therefore, the enemy is rebuked from touching
my harvest. In the name of Jesus, because I take care of God's
house, He will take care of my house. Lord, you say when I honor
You, You will honor me. I honor You with my tithe and offering.
Thank You that I am blessed coming in and going out; everything
my hand touches will prosper. I declare this by faith and it is so.
In Jesus' name, Amen.

Day 17

Not in My House

Luke 9:1-2

Then he called his twelve disciples together, and gave them power and authority over all devils, and to cure diseases. And he sent them to preach the kingdom of God, and to heal the sick.

Give the enemy his walking papers. Devil, this is your final notice that today you have to go. Take your imps with you as well for today is a new day for my family. And I have one more thing to say: don't waste your time coming back because the locks on my door have been changed. The blood of Jesus will watch over this house. Be gone.

Declaration:

Father, in the name of Jesus, I use the authority You have given me and today I command every attack against me and my family to be no more. Every disease I cut it off at the root. You have given me power over all the ability of the enemy. I declare that no weapons formed against me will prosper, and every tongue spoken against me will come to nothing. I declare this by faith in Jesus' name, Amen.

Day 18

It Is Settled

Psalm 119:89

Forever, O Lord, thy word is settled in heaven.

You're in the season of your life that there are certain things you have to settle. The word settled is defined as: resolved definitely and conclusively and to agree upon. Your faith in God and His Word is the gateway to your VICTORY. Settle it today that you will be faithful. You will walk by faith. You will tithe and give offering. You will walk in love with your spouse no matter what.

Declaration:

I declare by faith that this is my year of things being settled in my life. The day of going back and forward are over for me. Today I resolve definitely and conclusively and agree that I will walk by faith, that I will be faithful, and I will give. In the name of Jesus, I declare it is settled. Because it's settled in heaven, it's settled in my life. In the name of Jesus, I declare as Jesus is, so am I in this world. Thank your Father for the VICTORY. In Jesus' name, I declare this by faith. It is settled!

Day 19

Mind Cleansing

Proverbs 23:7

For as he thinketh in his heart, so is he: Eat and drink, saith he to thee; but his heart is not with thee.

You must on purpose guard the thoughts you are receiving. Believe it or not you will travel down the road that you visit the most in your mind. If you don't like the road that you are on, you have to change direction. You have to detox your mind from wrong images and thoughts. God has given us instruction in His Word on what to think about. It's time to change. See yourself out of debt, see yourself healed, see your child coming back to the Lord, see that promotion coming this year, see yourself in that car, see yourself in that new house. If you can see it you can have it.

Declaration:

I declare by faith that my mind is stayed on the word. I make a clean break from wrong thinking. In the name of Jesus, I have been given the mind of Christ. Therefore, I have the same thoughts that my heavenly Father has. His thoughts toward me are good. My mind is stayed on Him and I am in total peace. I choose to believe every word that God has said about me. In the name of Jesus, I win.

Day 20

Man Up

1 Peter 3:7

Likewise, ye husbands, dwell with them according to knowledge, giving honour unto the wife, as unto the weaker vessel, and as being heirs together of the grace of life; that your prayers be not hindered.

Hus*bands* you are the band that holds your family together. Your family needs you. There are instructions that have been handed down for husbands to follow. It's not up for debate. Husbands, God has given us the key to getting our prayers answered. We must treat our wives with respect and honor. There is a missing factor in this generation today where husbands are failing to respect their wives. However, God is raising up powerful husbands in these last days that will carry out the spirit and letter of this verse.

Declaration:

Father, In the name of Jesus, I honor and respect my wife. Therefore, my prayers will never fail. My wife and I love long and love strong. What you have joined together nothing or no one can tear apart. In the name of Jesus, I lift my wife up in prayer everyday so that she can carry out her assignment in this earth. In the name of Jesus, I cover her with love that she may always feel loved. I take my position now to man up and be the husband You have called me to be. In Jesus' name, Amen.

Day 21

Healing is Yours for the Taking

Isaiah 53:1-5 (ERV)

Who really believed what we heard? Who saw in it the Lord's great power? He was always close to the Lord. He grew up like a young plant, like a root growing in dry ground. There was nothing special or impressive about the way he looked, nothing we could see that would cause us to like him. People made fun of him, and even his friends left him. He was a man who suffered a lot of pain and sickness. We treated him like someone of no importance, like someone people will not even look at but turn away from in disgust. The fact is, it was our suffering he took on himself; he bore our pain. But we thought that God was punishing him, that God was beating him for something he did. But he was being punished for what we did. He was crushed because of our guilt. He took the punishment we deserved, and this brought us peace. We were healed because of his pain.

Healing belongs to you. Jesus died to secure your healing. The price has already been paid. So, take it by faith. It's yours for the taking.

Declaration:

I declare by faith that healing belongs to me. I take by faith what Jesus died for me to have. I am healed now. Surely, He carried my pain, therefore, I resist the pain in my body now. I am pain free, I am sickness free, I am disease free. Pain you must go. Sickness you must go. I curse the root of every pain and every sickness. Jesus was wounded for me. Therefore, I will live long and strong. My eyes will not be dimmed and my natural forces will not be weakened. I will live to be 120 or until Jesus returns. I am healed from every sickness and disease. My blood pressure is 120/80. My heart is strong and healthy. I take my healing now in Jesus' name, Amen.

Day 22

Stay in Faith

Psalm 112:7-8 (ERV)

They will not be afraid of bad news. They are confident because they trust in the Lord.

They remain confident and without fear, so they defeat their enemies.

With all of the things that are uncertain, there is one thing that is certain. And that is this: our God is faithful and He will not fail us. Our heart has to be fixed on the word and the promises of God. If not we will waiver back in our faith. The just shall live by faith. Faith is your way of living.

Declaration:

Father, in the name of Jesus, I declare that my confidence is in You and Your word. I will not be moved by what is going on around me. I am the just and I live by my faith. Faith is the location where all things are possible for me. Therefore, I will not move from my location of faith in You. I will remain confident and without any form of fear so that my enemies are defeated. My faith is the VICTORY that overcomes this world. In Jesus' name, I walk by faith and not by sight.

Day 23

Give Him Praise

Psalm 22:3 (ERV)

God, you are the Holy One. You sit as King upon the praises of Israel.

Psalm 22:3

But thou art holy, O thou that inhabitest the praises of Israel.

Praise is an awesome weapon that God has given us to use. But for some we rarely use it. God the Father gave you praise as a weapon to use to defeat the enemy. Jesus knew that we needed weapons to defeat the plots of the enemy. This is a fail proof system. There is an old saying: don't wait for the battle to be over, shout now. God inhabits the praise of His people. In other words, God dwells in the atmosphere where praise is taking place.

Declaration:

In the name of Jesus, I will praise the Lord at all times and His praise will forever be in my mouth. I will boast of the Lord's goodness all the days of my life. I declare that my praise will become the vehicle that will bring me into the presence of almighty God. There I will enter into His gates with thanksgiving, and into His court with praise, and I will be thankful unto Him, and bless His holy name. In Jesus' name, I have the VICTORY.

Day 24

Shout Grace to It

Zechariah 4:6-7

Then he answered and spake unto me, saying, This is the word of the Lord unto Zerubbabel, saying, Not by might, nor by power, but by my spirit, saith the Lord of hosts.

Who art thou, O great mountain? before Zerubbabel thou shalt become a plain: and he shall bring forth the headstone thereof with shoutings, crying, Grace, grace unto it.

The grace of God is God showing up in your life to empower you to do what you can't do in the natural. That should have happened; this should have taken place; I should have lost my mind when that occurred, but the grace of God showed up and made a way for me. Go ahead and shout grace to your mountain and your mountain will become plain.

Declaration:

In the name of Jesus, I shout grace to debt. I shout grace to sickness. I shout grace to the trouble on my job. I shout grace over my marriage. I shout grace over my family. I shout grace to every problem in my life. You are coming down now in Jesus' name, Amen. Grace be unto me.

Day 25

Make the Adjustment

Luke 18:18-27

And a certain ruler asked him, saying, Good Master, what shall I do to inherit eternal life?

And Jesus said unto him, Why callest thou me good? none is good, save one, that is, God.

Thou knowest the commandments, Do not commit adultery, Do not kill, Do not steal, Do not bear false witness, Honour thy father and thy mother.

And he said, All these have I kept from my youth up.

Now when Jesus heard these things, he said unto him, Yet lackest thou one thing: sell all that thou hast, and distribute unto the poor, and thou shalt have treasure in heaven: and come, follow me.

And when he heard this, he was very sorrowful: for he was very rich.

And when Jesus saw that he was very sorrowful, he said, How hardly shall they that have riches enter into the kingdom of God!

For it is easier for a camel to go through a needle's eye, than for a rich man to enter into the kingdom of God.

And they that heard it said, Who then can be saved?

And he said, The things which are impossible with men are possible with God.

Following Jesus always requires some type of adjustment in our lives. Whenever God speaks to your spirit about something, that is information that will reveal revelation for our invitation to make adjustments in our lives to God.

This is my story of making adjustments. I enjoy playing golf so much that I wanted this new ping driver. I read all the reviews about how far you can hit with it. So, I ended up buying one. This club comes with certain tools you need so you can make adjustments on the head and get the ultimate shot you want. But I never used the tools that came with the club. I played with it a couple of time and didn't play well with it at all. I asked the Lord why couldn't I hit this club. He said, "You didn't make the necessary adjustments. There's nothing wrong with the club. It's designed to do what it was made to do. However, you failed to make the adjustments." I wonder how many times we fail to make adjustment in our lives. God has already prepared everything for us to enjoy.

Declaration:

Father, in the name of Jesus I make the necessary adjustment in my life starting today. Because of these adjustments in my life it will bring revelation and knowledge that will flow into my born-again spirit. I declare that there is nothing impossible for You to do. I take You at Your word. I declare this by faith. In Jesus' name, Amen.

Day 26

Everything Will Be Alright

2 Kings 4:25-26 (ERV)

The woman went to Mount Carmel to get the man of God. The man of God saw the Shunammite woman coming from far away and said to his servant Gehazi, "Look, there's the Shunammite woman! Please run now to meet her! Say to her, 'Are you all right? Is your husband all right? Is the child all right?'" She answered, "Everything is all right."

This is such an amazing story. How did she summon the faith to declare it is well when she knew that it wasn't? It was her faith in what the man of God had spoken to her. This woman of faith held her dying son that was given to her by God. She said nothing to no one but still found the faith to say everything is all right. In everything let your answer be like this Shunammite woman: everything is all right.

Declaration:

I declare that all is well with me. All is well with my health, and every word that God has spoken over me will be fulfilled in my life. I call every dead thing back to life now in the name of Jesus. Father, I declare that everything is all right in me. I release my faith, and say with boldness ALL IS WELL. In Jesus' name, Amen.

Day 27

God Has Your Back

Exodus 14:14 (ERV)

You will not have to do anything but stay calm. The Lord will do the fighting for you.

What do we do when our faith has been challenge? Obtaining victory in our lives is very important to each of us. I have great news for you, when you made Jesus Christ your Lord and savior, you now have access to the greatest warrior who ever lived and has never lost a battle. The Bible teaches us that He is a man of war. The Lord will fight for you. In other words, God has your back.

Declaration:

Father, in the name of Jesus, I choose not to worry about this problem in my life. I declare that I maintain my trust in You and Your word to bring to pass what I ask for. I will not grow weary while well doing because my breakthrough is at hand. I employ patience in my life to allow you to fight on my behalf. Therefore, it is by faith that I will not be moved. In the name of Jesus, I thank You for having my back and You are doing the fighting for me. In Jesus' name, Amen.

Day 28

It's On the Way

2 Peter 3:9 (ERV)

The Lord is not being slow in doing what he promised—the way some people understand slowness. But God is being patient with you. He doesn't want anyone to be lost. He wants everyone to change their ways and stop sinning.

In our walk of faith, it seems like what God has promised is slow in coming. Many times, we can't see it, touch it, or feel it. So, the enemy will plant a seed of doubt in our mind to get us to believe that what God has promised will not come to pass. Here is God's word to us: He is not slow in doing what He promised. God is always faithful. What God has promised us always requires a step of faith.

Declaration:

Father, in the name of Jesus, I declare that something good is about to happen to me. No matter how long it takes for that promise to manifest in my life, I still trust You. Every thought that says it is not going to happen, I refute that thought now in the name of Jesus. Father, all of your promises to me are yes and amen. Therefore, I believe Your word to me will come to pass. Thank you for teaching me to be patient. In Jesus' name, Amen.

Day 29

This is Your Turnaround Moment

Jeremiah 29:13-14 (MSG)

When you come looking for me, you'll find me.

Yes, when you get serious about finding me and want it more than anything else, I'll make sure you won't be disappointed. God's Decree.

"I'll turn things around for you. I'll bring you back from all the countries into which I drove you"—God's Decree—"bring you home to the place from which I sent you off into exile. You can count on it.

Declare that whatever your situation may be, God can turn it around. You have endured a lot and it seems like there is no end in sight. But I want you to know that the God we serve can do anything. There is nothing too hard for our God. The word *turn* means to cause to rotate, to change the position of, to move so that the upper side become the under, to take a new direction. The word *turnaround* is defined as a shift or reverse of a trend or procedure. You need to start declaring that there is a shift that is about to take place in your life.

Declaration:

Father, in the name of Jesus, I declare that this is my year that I will become serious about my walk with You. And because of that, You said I will not be disappointed and that You will not fail to fulfill my expectation and desire that I have in my heart. In the name of Jesus, You can be counted on to do what You said. Therefore, I release my faith and declare that this is my turnaround moment. In Jesus' name, Amen.

Day 30

Embrace the Father's Love

Luke 15:17-24 (ERV)

The son realized that he had been very foolish. He thought, 'All my father's hired workers have plenty of food. But here I am, almost dead because I have nothing to eat. I will leave and go to my father. I will say to him: Father, I have sinned against God and have done wrong to you. I am no longer worthy to be called your son. But let me be like one of your hired workers.' So he left and went to his father.

While the son was still a long way off, his father saw him coming and felt sorry for him. So he ran to him and hugged and kissed him. The son said, 'Father, I have sinned against God and have done wrong to you. I am no longer worthy to be called your son.'

But the father said to his servants, 'Hurry! Bring the best clothes and put them on him. Also, put a ring on his finger and good sandals on his feet. And bring our best calf and kill it so that we can celebrate with plenty to eat. My son was dead, but now he is alive again! He was lost, but now he is found!' So they began to have a party.

This is a wonderful story of a father's love. It's important for us to know that our heavenly Father indeed loves us. No matter what we have done or will do, it will never change the way God cares about us. We are His children and He loves us. You have to settle the issue that God loves you. When we discover how much He loves us, our believing becomes easy. I love the fact that when the father ran out to embrace his son, not once did he ask him where he had been. I'm sure he smelled like the swine but it did not matter to the father. The father was simply overjoyed at the fact that his son who was lost was now found. God wants you to know that whatever you may have gone through, He is waiting for you to come back home. Embrace His love for you today and He will take care of the smell.

Declaration:

Father in the name of Jesus, I embrace your love for me. Forgive me for leaving my first love. Today, I make a quality decision that nothing will separate me from You. Knowing that You died for me shows Your love for me. Thank You for never leaving me when I was doing things my own way. Your love kept chasing me down. In the name of Jesus, I know that You love me and that You care for me. I don't know where I would be if it wasn't for Your love. I embrace Your love for me from this day forward. In Jesus' name, Amen.

Day 31

Year of Great Victories

John 16:33 (ERV)

I have told you these things so that you can have peace in me. In this world you will have troubles. But be brave! I have defeated the world!

John 16:33 (NLT)

I have told you all this so that you may have peace in me. Here on earth you will have many trials and sorrows. But take heart, because I have overcome the world.

What the Lord has spoken belongs to us. God, the Father, has great plans in store for those who have made Jesus their Lord and Savior. The timing is now for us to release our faith for great victories in our lives. God's timing is now for Him to release certain things for us. However, in order to receive what He is releasing in this season, we are required to operate in faith. Jesus has already defeated this world's system. When you can already see the victory God has provided by His amazing grace, you can face the challenges that the world bring because you have peace in your heart, faith in your God, and confidence in His finished work.

Declaration:

In the name of Jesus, I thank You for defeating the world so that I can walk in total victory. I believe and receive what You have spoken to me. I open my heart to all You want to do in and through me. Come what may, I believe I am an overcomer. You have already defeated the enemy. Therefore, I boldly declare that as Jesus is, so am I in this world. Father, I release my faith now, and declare that the devil is defeated in my life. I pray this in faith, believing it's already done. In Jesus' name, Amen.

Prayer of Salvation

God is not mad at you! He isn't counting your sins and holding them against you. He wants so much to have a personal relationship with you that He sent Jesus, His only Son, to shed His blood, die on the cross, and then be raised from the dead. He did all that so that you can be set free from the bondage of sin and the fear of death and enter into eternal life.

Romans 10:9-10 says, *That if thou shalt confess with thy mouth the Lord Jesus, and shalt believe in thine heart that God hath raised him from the dead, thou shalt be saved. For with the heart man believeth unto righteousness; and with the mouth confession is made unto salvation.*

Confess this by faith:

Dear God, I want to be a part of your family. You said in Your Word that if I acknowledge that You raised Jesus from the dead, and that I accept Him as my Lord and Savior, I would be saved. So God, I now say that I believe You raised Jesus from the dead and that He is alive and well. I accept Him now as my personal Lord and Savior. I accept my salvation from sin right now. I am now saved. Jesus is my Lord. Jesus is my Savior. Thank you, Father God, for forgiving me, saving me, and giving me eternal life with You. In Jesus' name, Amen!

If you just prayed this prayer for the first time, we welcome you to the family of God! We would love to send you some free literature to help you in your walk with God. You can visit our website at: www.shegogministries.org

Love,

Pastors Carl & Valarie Shegog

Word Alive Family Worship Center
The Place Where Your VICTORY Begins

About the Author

Carl, along with his wife Valarie Shegog, are the pastors and teachers of Word Alive Family Worship Center in Alexandria, Virginia. They began fulfilling God's call to the five-fold ministry while stationed in Schweinfurt Germany

Pastors Carl and Valarie's heart's desire is to rebuild, reconstruct, and restore.

To contact the author for speaking engagements, conferences, book tours and signings, write

Visit www.shegogministries.com
E-mail: wordaliveministry@cfaith.com

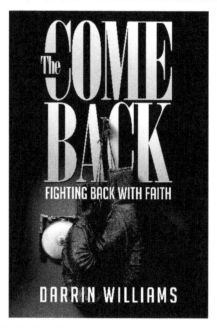

Other Authors by

COOKE PUBLISHING HOUSE

Sometimes getting up early doesn't always have to be a chore; it can sometimes be a delightful adventure that will shape and change your life forever. Walk with Rolinda Butler in Early Morning Visitor as she navigates you through a journey of spiritual discovery and a closer relationship with the Holy Spirit.

ISBN: 978-0-9979923-0-4

For more information, visit
www.earlymorningvisitor.com

CPSIA information can be obtained
at www.ICGtesting.com
Printed in the USA
BVOW11s1646070617

486135BV00001B/1/P